Came a Dealer in Dreams

A Play

Noel Scott

SAMUEL FRENCH

FOUNDED 1830

SAMUELFRENCH-LONDON.CO.UK
SAMUELFRENCH.COM

CHARACTERS

King Rum-ti-too
Prosecuting Counsel
Defending Counsel
Executioner
Mrs Everymother
Sleep
Compère
Two Actors (who double as **Guards**)
Crowd

The action takes place in the courtroom of the King's castle

NOTE ON COSTUMES

The Guards are fitted with suitable medieval weapons. The Crowd wears garments suited for a "fairy-tale" story. Counsels for Prosecution and Defence can wear gowns and wigs. Sleep has a cloak, possibly of many colours: he has to wave and weave the garment to bewitch the other characters.

CAME A DEALER IN DREAMS

A Courtroom in the castle

When the play starts the CURTAINS *are closed. Behind are assembled the cast in position*

From each side an Actor enters. They take up positions C *and speak alternate lines, each following on to give point to the rhymes*

One There's a funny sort of rumour and it's creeping through the town;

Two And no-one seems to know just what the source is.

One Yes, they've heard it in the country, all through village, dale and town—

Two And it's even reached his Majesty's armed forces!

One Yes, it's really most mysterious—

Two   —the King is quite perturbed;

One For the peace of all his subjects—

Two   —and himself—

One Has been disturbed.

Two By a most peculiar personage who's wandering through the land,

One Performing—sort of—well, you know, it's hard to understand just what the fellow's doing—

Two For rumours vary so!

One It's this—

Two Or that—

One Or rather more—

Two I'm positive!

One Oh, no!

Two Well, don't let's quarrel what it is, there's one thing very clear;

One That personage is now on trial from all the noise I hear!

The CURTAINS *open to reveal the court in session*

The two Actors of the Introduction bow and depart into the wings

The King is seated on his throne. He is straightforward and irritable.

*Nearby stand the Prosecuting Counsel, gruff and hard-hearted, and
the Defending Counsel, smooth and easy-going, and the Executioner,
who is down-to-earth but soft-hearted beneath his fierce exterior.
Among the crowd stands Mrs Everymother: she sounds Irish and is
warm, likeable and poetic. The Compère steps forward from the
assembled crowd*

Compère   Good friends, I'm here to introduce our play
                 Which opens in this castle here, today.
                 And all the characters in turn I'll take;
                 First—(*he points to the King*)—King Rum-ti-too
                     of Wide Awake.
King   Ah! Rum-ti-too! A monarch bold and fierce;
                 Who's ruled the land of Wide Awake for years.
                 A land where people work all day and night
                 With might and main—and then with main and
                     might!
Compère   A most important trial is due to start,
                 So next—the Prosecuting Counsel's part!
Prosecuting Counsel
                 That's me! A stern-faced, fearsome, shocking fellow!
                 And many a criminal's quaked to hear me bellow!
                 You should see them wilt
                 When I prove their guilt—
                 In fact, they turn quite yellow!
Compère   But justice says, before complaints commence,
                 The prisoner needs a Counsel for Defence.
Defending Counsel That's me, folks! And you won't find a
    better chap for the job! Kind-hearted; good-natured—see the
    best in everybody—that's me! You watch, I'll have the
    prisoner whiter than white in no time!
Compère (*pointing to the Executioner*)
                 And this grim creature with his axe—
                 I think I'll ask *him* to tell you the facts!
Executioner Yes; I'm the Executioner; ready for work;
                 A job I've never been known to shirk!
                 And many's the wrong 'un who's come a cropper
                 When I starts a-swingin' me little—choppah!
Compère   And round the court-room; massed in deep array,
                 The people wait to hear this trial today.

> For never has there been so strange a case
> As this one in the Land of Wide Awake!

King Bring him in! Bring in the villain who dares upset my kingdom! Executioner, is your axe ready?

Executioner Ay, ay, Y'Majesty! Sharp as an east wind!

King Axellent—I mean, excellent! Where is he? Let's have a look at him and . . .

The King breaks off as the prisoner—Sleep, dignified, noble, poetic—is led in between two Guards. So dignified is the newcomer that a murmer of wonder arises from the people in court

So there you are! And about time, too! This throne gets harder every minute! Why can't I have a cushion to sit on?

Defending Counsel It's gone to the cleaners, M'Lud!

King Gone to the cleaners! Gone to the cleaners! Oh, well, never mind! Now, sirrah, I condemn you to be . . .

Prosecuting Counsel Please, please, Your Majesty; you can't conduct the case like that; at least, not until I've had my say as Prosecuting Counsel!

King Wha—what? Oh, ah. Yes, all right; but get on with it. I don't suppose it will make any difference!

Prosecuting Counsel Prisoner at the bar; it seems you have been wandering through the land of Wide Awake, and practising the wiles of witchcraft . . .

King What craft?

Prosecuting Counsel No, witchcraft, Y'Majesty. As you well know, in the land of Wide Awake we work by day and by night, without break or rest.

King And very right and proper! Whoever heard of anything else?

Prosecuting Counsel Ha-ha, but this rascal has, Your Majesty, when you hear what he's been doing! At the hour of sunset he creeps up to people and whispers a spell in their ears—waves his cloak—and what happens?

The Crowd Yes, yes, what happens? Tell us! Tell us!

Prosecuting Counsel These people—these harmless citizens of Wide Awake hurry home and fall into a strange trance! And never does the spell break until the hour of sunrise next day! The people utter cries of wonder and amazement. And what is more, the people who are thus bewitched discover there is no escape from the spell. It falls on them each night, and they never work, nor eat nor talk! In fact, they lie there just like lumps of wood!

King Lumps of wood! Lumps of wood! What does he think I am—a king or a carpenter? Lumps of wood? Where should I be with an army of wooden soldiers? Though, of course, I could—er—drill them easily—er—drill them ... Oh, never mind—if you can't see the joke!

Prosecuting Counsel Ah, Your Majesty, you would not joke if only you saw the people who are affected! And it's not only the people—the birds in the trees, the cattle in the field, the sheep in the fold—they all come under his spell!

King Nay, by the hump of the dromedary, this is too much! By the hip of the potamus, the villain must suffer! He shall be executed at once! Executioner, do your duty!

Executioner Ay, ay, Your Honour, I'm ready ...

Defending Counsel Stop! You can't do that!

King Oh, and why can't I?

Defending Counsel Because, sire, the case must be properly conducted! You must hear what the prisoner has to say; or rather, what I have to say on his behalf!

King Oh, well; I've had to listen to him—(*pointing to the Prosecuting Counsel*)—so I might as well suffer your chatter. It won't make any difference. (*He wriggles*) Only don't be long; this throne gets harder every minute!

Defending Counsel Well, well, we must see! Ladies and gentlemen, rarely has it been my privilege to talk to such a distinguished audience; such a good-looking crowd of people, as I see before me now. Of course, you mustn't believe all you hear about this poor fellow here! (*He gestures to the prisoner*) Just look at him! A more harmless person never trod the streets of Wide Awake since the pavements were laid! Magic spells! Rubbish! I've spoken to several people who've been—er—affected, and what did they say?

The Crowd Yes, yes, what did they say? Tell us! Tell us!

Defending Counsel They said they never felt better in all their life! They work twice as hard, and actually look forward to sunset when they are bewitched—er—that is, when they actually undergo this change!

King Incredible! Unbelievable!

Prosecuting Counsel Impossible! Ridiculous!

Defending Counsel And the babies love him! And so do the mothers!

Mrs Everymother Sure, and the gentleman speaks me very thoughts!

King Who—what—bless my whiskers, who is this woman?

Mrs Everymother Me name, sorr, is Mrs Everymother. And I speak for all the mothers in this land of Wide Awake when I say ye've no cause to be hard on the poor fellow!

Defending Counsel Exactly, madam. And will you please tell His Majesty how this prisoner helps you and other mothers in the land.

Mrs Everymother Your Honour shall hear it straight away! Y'see, sorr, 'tis our babies, when they hear the wonder of his words! You watch their lovely eyes closing like buds at eventide—and the sweetness of their smiles lingering on, as if the fairy folk had painted them there! And while the little ones lie there so quiet, it's straight to work for us mothers, and our cooking and cleaning is done in no time!

Defending Counsel Now there you are, Your Majesty! See what a great help he is to all these busy mothers?

King Oh, worry, worry, worry! I just don't know what to say! Here, Mr Prisoner-at-the-Bar or whatever your name is, what d'you mean by coming here and upsetting the laws and the land of Wide Awake?

Sleep Who I am you wish to know;
      Whence I come and whither I go.
      My name to you is a name unknown,
      As by your strange behaviour shown!
      My name is SLEEP!

The Crowd (*like an echo*) Sleep? Sleep? Sleep?

Sleep I steal o'er the world when daylight is ended;
      In the wake of the sunset my long path is wended.
      The gleam of the stars is the lamp on my road;
      And a bag full of dreams I bear for a load.
         My spells are the charms that bring slumber and rest
         To the child in the cot and the bird in the nest.
         I whisper sweet thoughts till their eyelids close
         And leave them a dream for happy repose.
      On young and old I weave my spell
      And all the daytime cares dispel;

In towns and hamlets, caves and hills
I wave my cloak—(*he moves his cloak*)—as fancy wills.
For in this garment, magic lies
To close the lids on weary eyes.
  But in this land of Wide Awake
  Such things have never been the case!
  And this I mean to alter!
King You—you mean to do whatt!
Sleep Your subjects have long been free of my cares
  And lived in a very strange state of affairs,
  By toiling all day and toiling all night . . .
  And nonsense like this I mean to set right.
    In fact I am determined to make
    New laws in the land of Wide Awake!

A murmur of alarm

  So, from dusk until night dies,
  In this land, shall none rise
  For work or for playtime.
  I thus do intend
  Such nonsense shall end
  And slumber shall reign until daytime!
    So—high or low and young and old
  Whatever be your station:
    Now learn to do as you are told.
  My spell is on your nation!
  And you—and you—and you—and you—
  Will find out your mistake;
  This land no longer shall be called—
  The land of Wide Awake!

A murmur of wonder from the Crowd

Defending Counsel So you see, Your Majesty!
Prosecuting Counsel And now you see, Your Majesty!
King What d'you think you are—a couple of echoes? Oh, yes;
  I see all right! This—this rascal comes here and decides to
  alter the laws, just like that! And if *I* want to make a new law it
  has to go before the Council of State half a dozen times; then
  the people pull it to pieces, and the tinker, tailor, soldier *and*
  sailor all have a word to say, and it gets so changed, I hardly

recognize it! But you—you Prisoner-at-the-Bar or whatever your name is, you have the nerve to talk about making new laws as if it's as easy as making a treacle tart! Why—I—I—why, I'm so angry I hardly know who I am ...

Defending Counsel Allow me, sire, you are King Rum-ti-too of Wide Awake Land!

King Idiot! Of course I know who I am! You know I don't mean everything I say—I mean, I don't always tell the truth—I mean—why do you keep bothering me and flustering me?

Defending Counsel Nobody wants to fluster you, sire. I only want you to let the prisoner go free. Besides, just think what a blessing this spell could be when some old bore is talking and he drops off to sleep in the middle of his tale!

King Hm, ah, yes, there *is* something to be said for that side of the case! Er, at times, the Queen does get a little ... Hrrh, ah, yes, quite! Here, Mr Sleep or whatever your name is, can I work the magic charm?

Sleep The charm to men I may not tell.

      I—I alone can work the spell!

Prosecuting Counsel There you are! Only he can do it! And has Your Majesty thought what it will mean if people go to sleep every night? We shall no longer be the powerful nation of Wide Awake. Half Awake will be more like it! And think of the beds and blankets and pillows we shall need!

King Jumping giraffes! This gets worse every minute! Here, Executioner, you're a sensible sort of fellow; what d'*you* think I should do?

Executioner Well, Y'Majesty, I'm all for speaking plain and straightforward like. What's the good of having a nice, bright, shiny weaping—(*waving his axe*)—like this if I'm never going to use it? I haven't had an execution for years and years, and all the time I'm a-polishing and sharpening me little choppah till you could use it as a mirror to shave *in* or a razor to shave *with*! So, if you ask me—which you do—I say—execute him!

Prosecuting Counsel Hurrah! Hurrah!

Defending Counsel Shame! Shame!

Mrs Everymother No, no, we won't let you do it! Oh, the melody of his voice when he speaks! 'Tis all the beauty of the world in sound. I can hear the ceaseless murmur of bees on a summer's noon—the low of distant herds—the clip and slap of wavelets on a lake . . .

Defending Counsel The soothing surge of the sea on starlit shores . . .

Mrs Everymother Ay, Your Majesty, and the hiss of the kettle on the hob and the measured march of minutes from the clock! You must spare him, sorr!

King Stuff and nonsense—and likewise nuff and stonsense! What's the fellow done to you all? Has he bewitched you with his voice? Well, he's not going to win me over with his soft whisperings! Fellow, I order you to be executed at once, right now, on the spot, and no arguing!

A general cry of dismay

Sleep You bring me to this court for trial:
I meet your charges with denial!
So take my answer!
'Tis for your gain and for your good . . .

King Oh, stop him before he gets going again! And this throne gets harder every minute! Guards, seize him at once!

The Guards step forward but Sleep waves his cloak in an intricate pattern while he speaks

Sleep Then you shall see!
With a wave of my hand and a sweep of my cloak—
And you'll sadly regret that you ever spoke!

As the cloak ripples the Guards pause; rub their eyes and stretch their arms and yawn. Slowly they kneel and gently lay down their swords. Then they settle into different postures of sleep. A murmur of wonder arises at the picture. The King leaps to his feet

King Quick, Executioner! Chop off his head before he bewitches us all!

Executioner Ay, ay, sire! (*He leaps forward and starts to raise his axe, but pauses as Sleep waves his cloak*) Oooohh! I think I'll have to wait a bit, Y'Majesty! This axe do feel a bit—sort of heavy! I'll have to sit down a bit, if you don't mind! Another day, perhaps! D'you mind if I rest my head and—and think it over . . . (*His voice fades into a snore as he sits and leans his back against the throne*)

King You—you villain! D'you see what you've done!
Sleep I do. And be assured, before I go,
        That others will be treated so!
        Soldiers and servants—and King, as well—
        Will all come under my magic spell.
            I mean it when I make a law,
            And you shall obey it—for evermore!

Sleep waves his cloak and the whole court falls asleep. The Prisoner looks affectionately at his new-won subjects. With a noble smile he glides away as—

the CURTAINS *close*

FURNITURE AND PROPERTY LIST

On stage: Throne on rostrum

LIGHTING PLOT

Property fittings required: nil
Interior. A castlc courtroom
To open: Spots on front curtains
Cue 1:   As Curtains open   (Page 1)
                Bring up general interior lighting to full

MADE AND PRINTED IN GREAT BRITAIN BY
LATIMER TREND & COMPANY LTD PLYMOUTH
MADE IN ENGLAND

9 780573 152115